P9-ARP-256

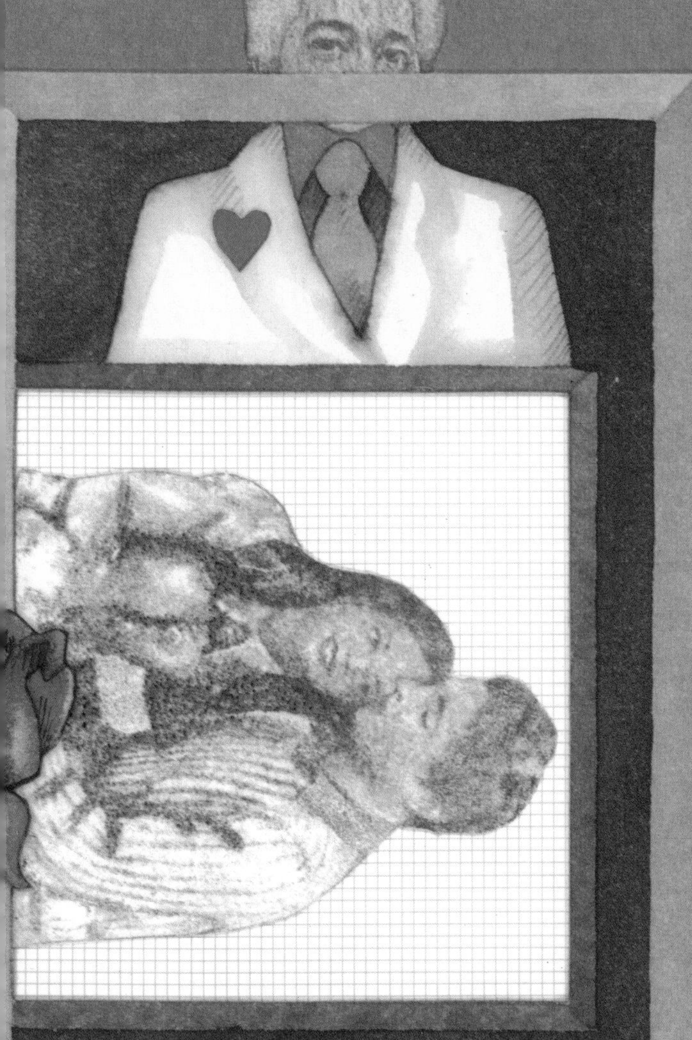

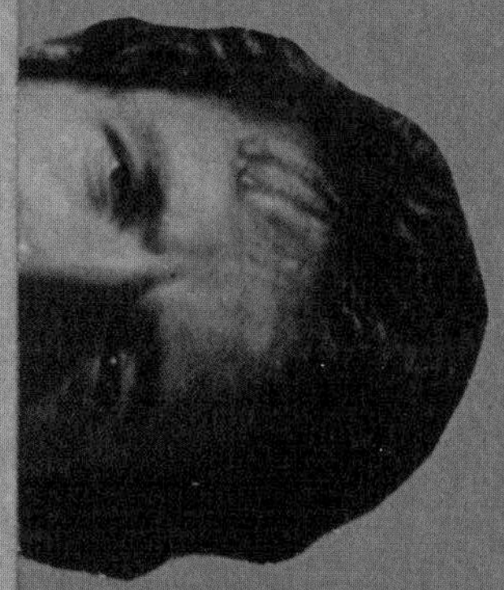

overmyer

To Otis,
From [illegible signature]

I Am My Brother

Written by Peter Seymour
Illustrated by Donni Giambrone,
Alex Gsoell, Jay Johnson,
John Overmyer, David Miles
and David Welty

Hallmark Crown Editions

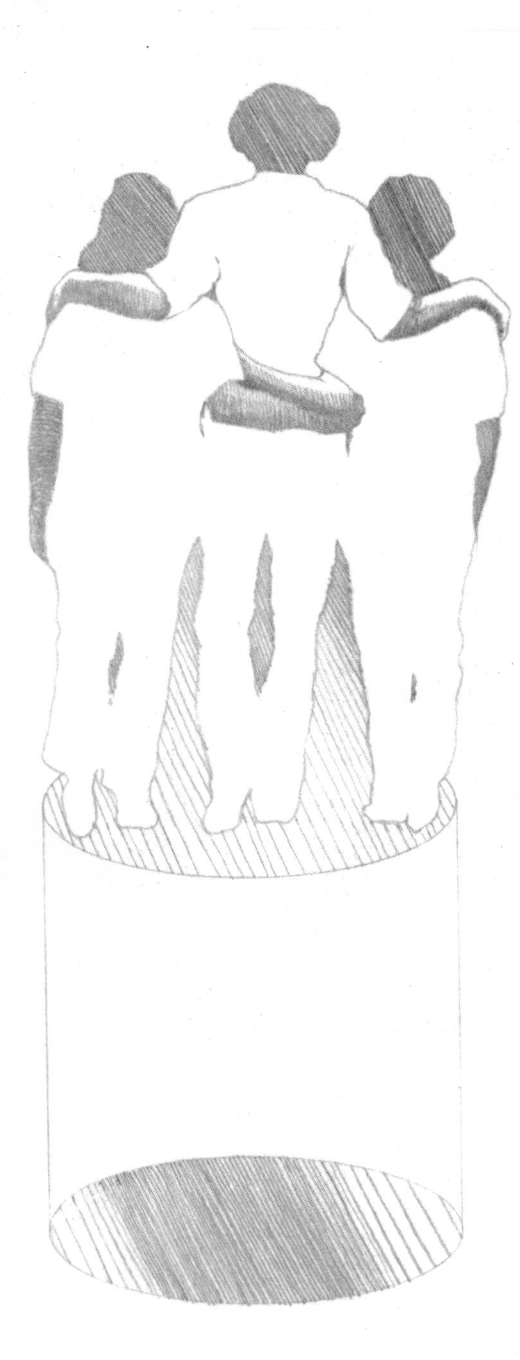

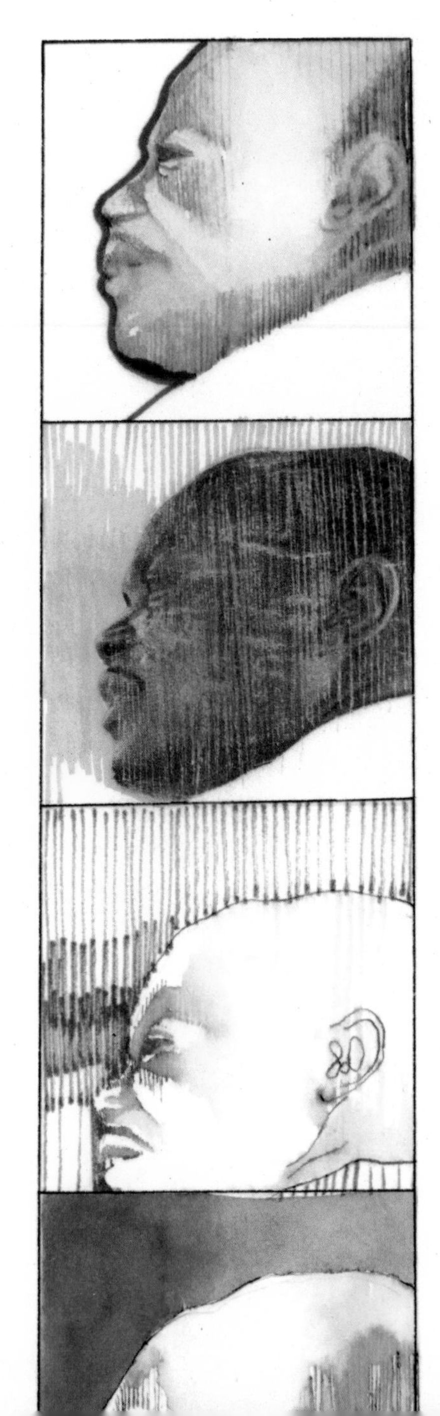

Printed in the United States of America.
Library of Congress Catalog Card Number: 76-187755.
Standard Book Number: 87529-279-8.

I am my brother...and my brother is me.

Ralph Waldo Emerson

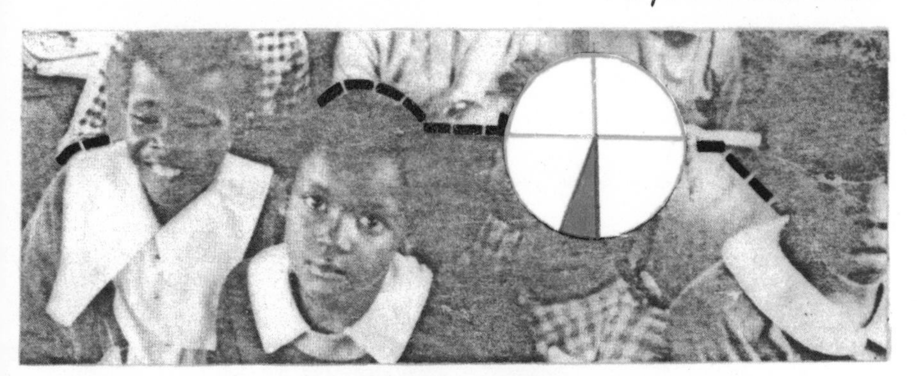

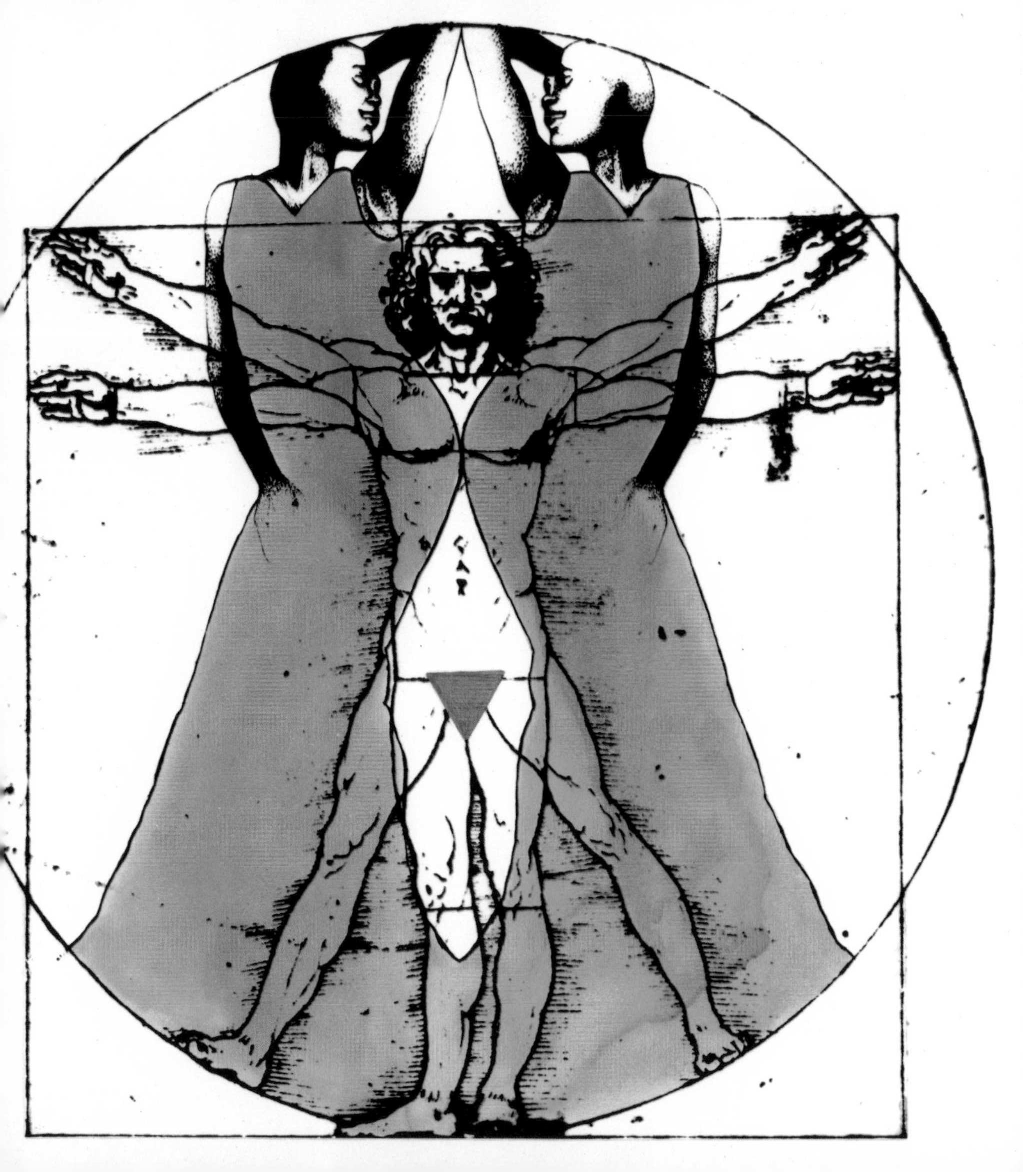

Within us all, beneath the layers of inhibitions

that come with growing up...

...shielding our feelings against hurt...

...a love for fellow man does exist...

...perhaps only as an ember...

...but it can--and does--

spark

glow

illuminate...

...drawing others in their need to us...

...pulling us to others in our wish for oneness.

In the fractured world of people...

alienated

distrustful

unsure

hurt...

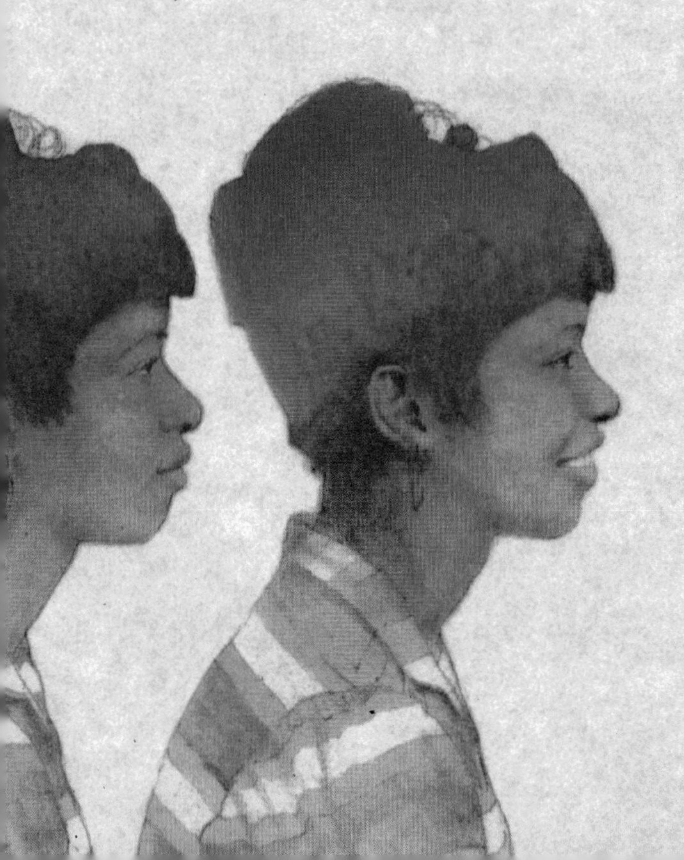

...love *is*.

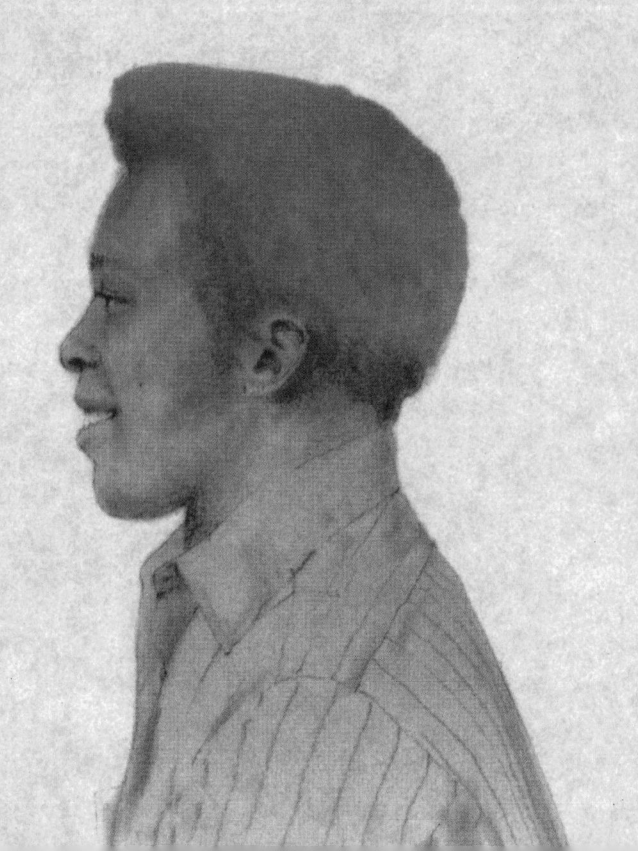

How else could we explain the moments of longing...

...the trembling within...

...the sad pangs for something lost...

...and the sudden leap of the spirit

for something found...

...the burst of joy when we look

into another's eyes

and see our common spirit?

It must be:

I am my brother...

and my brother is me.

For we are one

and cannot separate common feelings...

thoughts

dreams

of life.

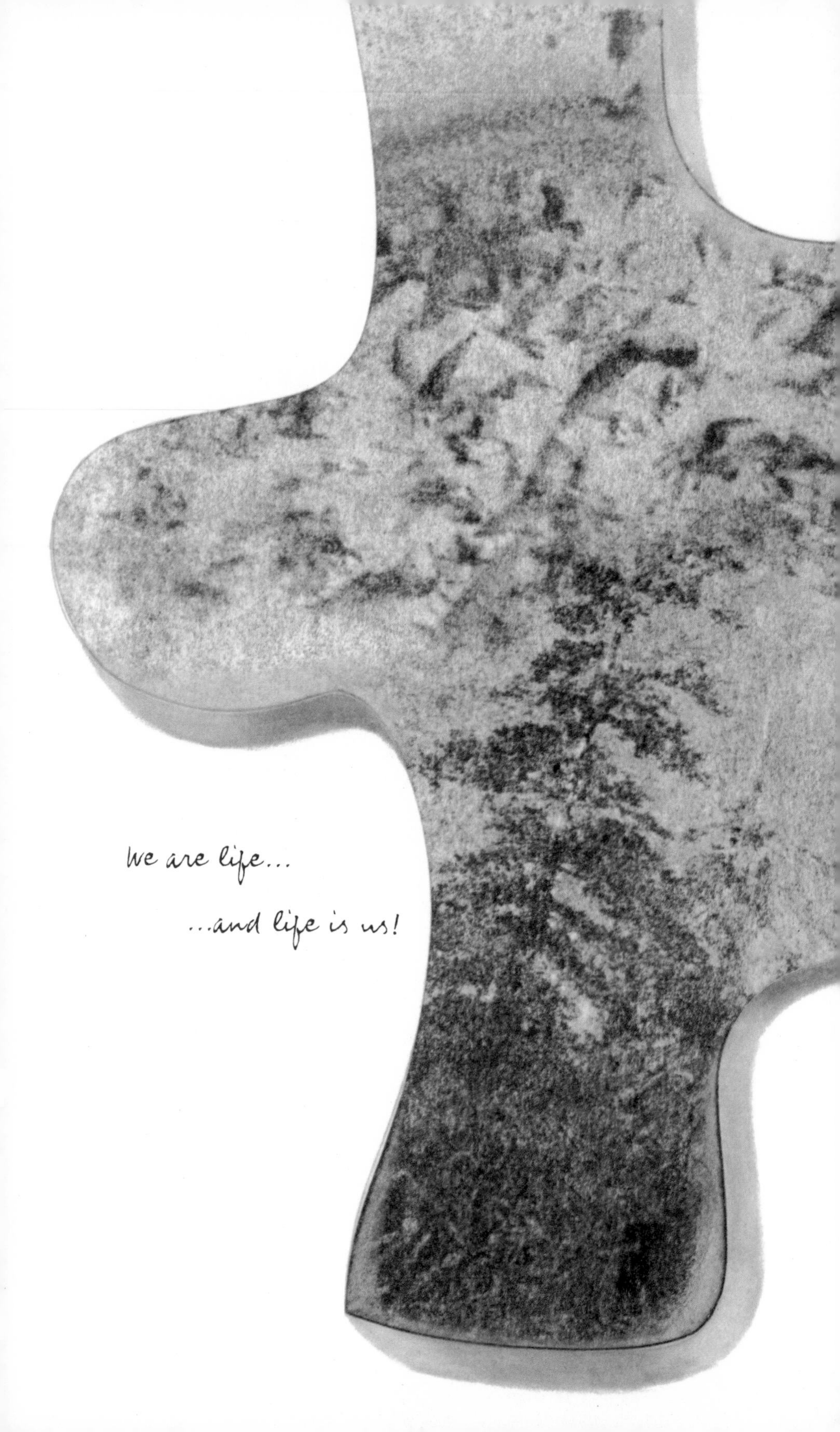

We are life...

...and life is us!

THE VALUE OF THIS CERTIFICATE IS
THREE DOLLARS
3
3

Life is people...

...not such things as

buildings, cars, washing machines, roast beef...

50
JACKPOT
25
donni

...life is breathing, smiling, laughing, crying, singing...

...the anger, fear, joy, compassion...

...life is the <u>love</u> that reaches out...

...building bridges across gulfs of uncertainty...

...to touch

hands

hearts

souls...

...in the experience of union.

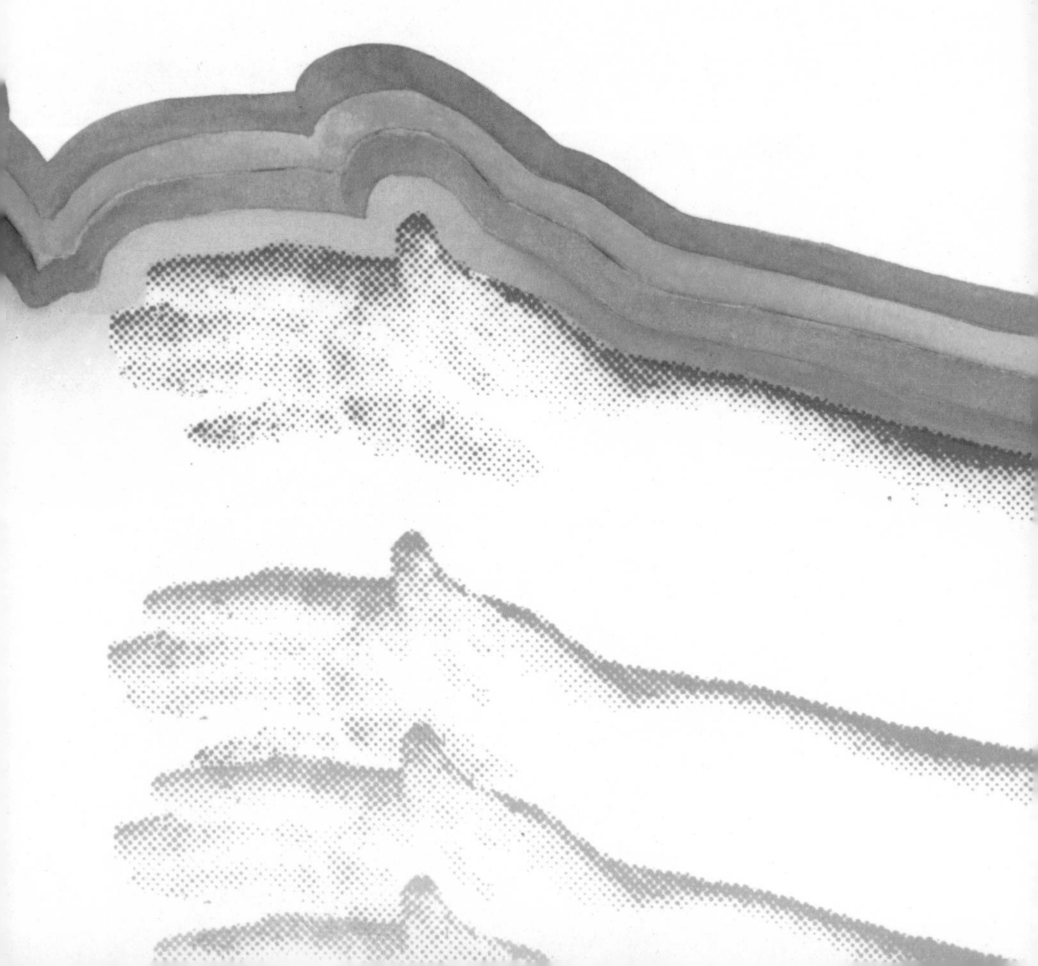

Few have said it better than John Donne--

"No man is an island...

...any man's death diminishes me,

because I am involved in mankind."

J. JOHNSON
1907–19

and Winfield Townley Scott--

"No man's creation

but enlarges me."

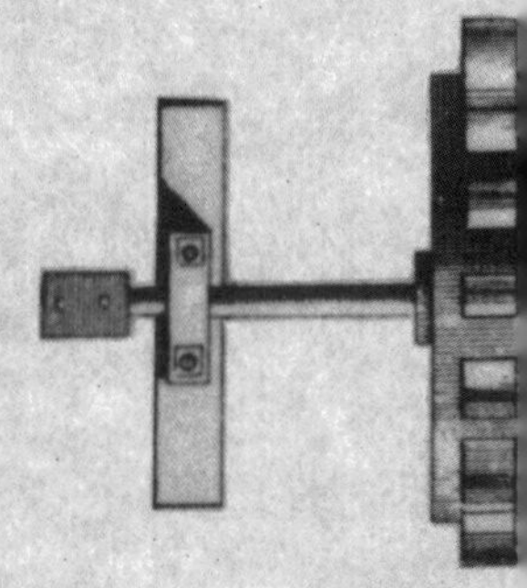

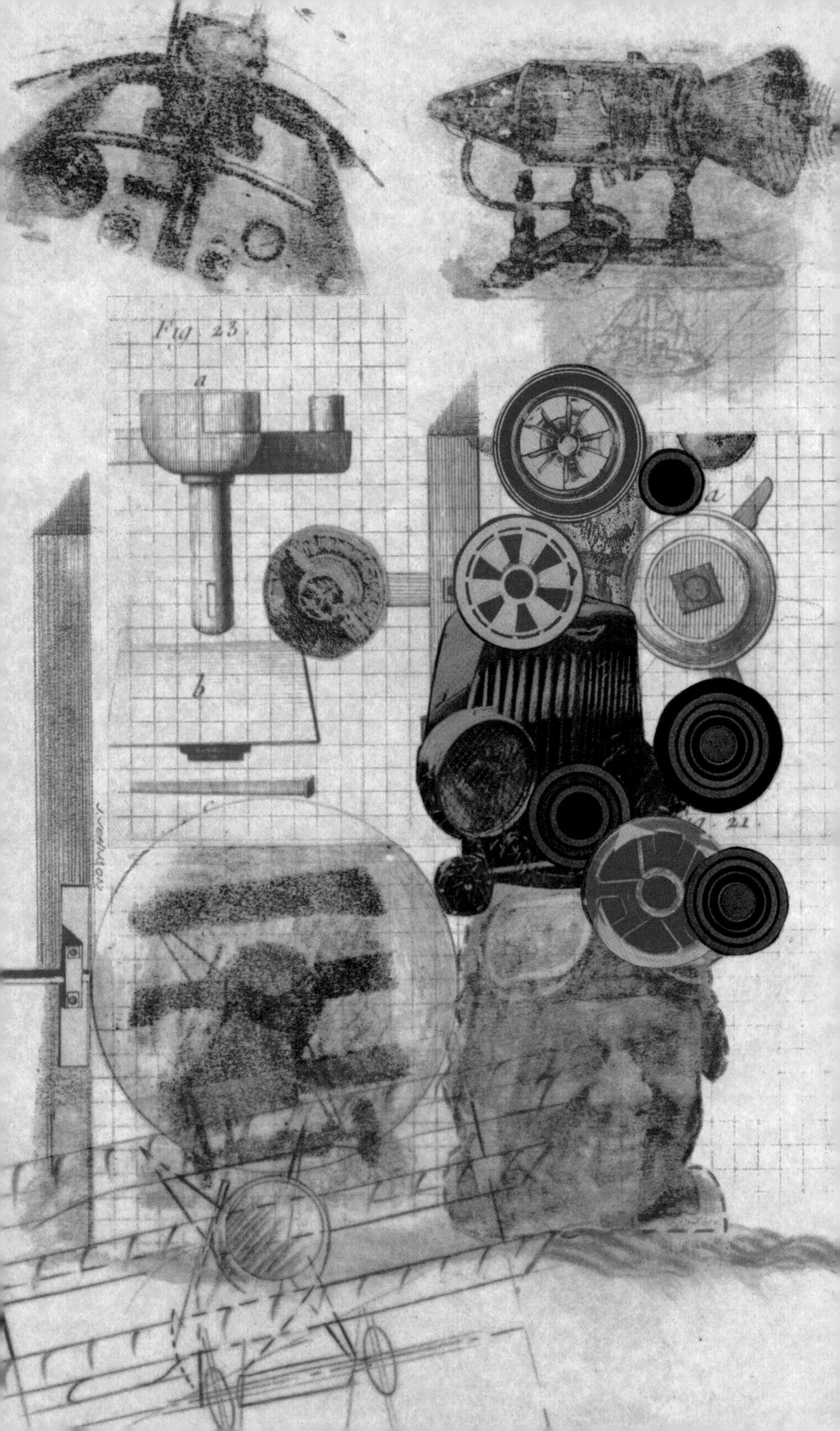
Fig 23
a
b
c
a
Fig 21

If, then, we believe
in the goodness of ourselves...
...we will believe in the goodness of others...

...for all are equal in their humanness...

...all possess inner beauty

not always seen on the surface...

...all are masked sometimes

with silence

arrogance

anger.

thus we cannot judge the package

by its wrappings...

...we can only accept the contents

as having value.

To care about others gives life meaning...

...if we speak to strangers...

...and listen, too...

...if we aren't afraid to show that we care...

J. JOHNSON

David Welty

...then we find that what we give to the lives

of others returns to our own...

David Welty

...and love begets love.

"Love a man," Dostoevski wrote, "even in his sin--

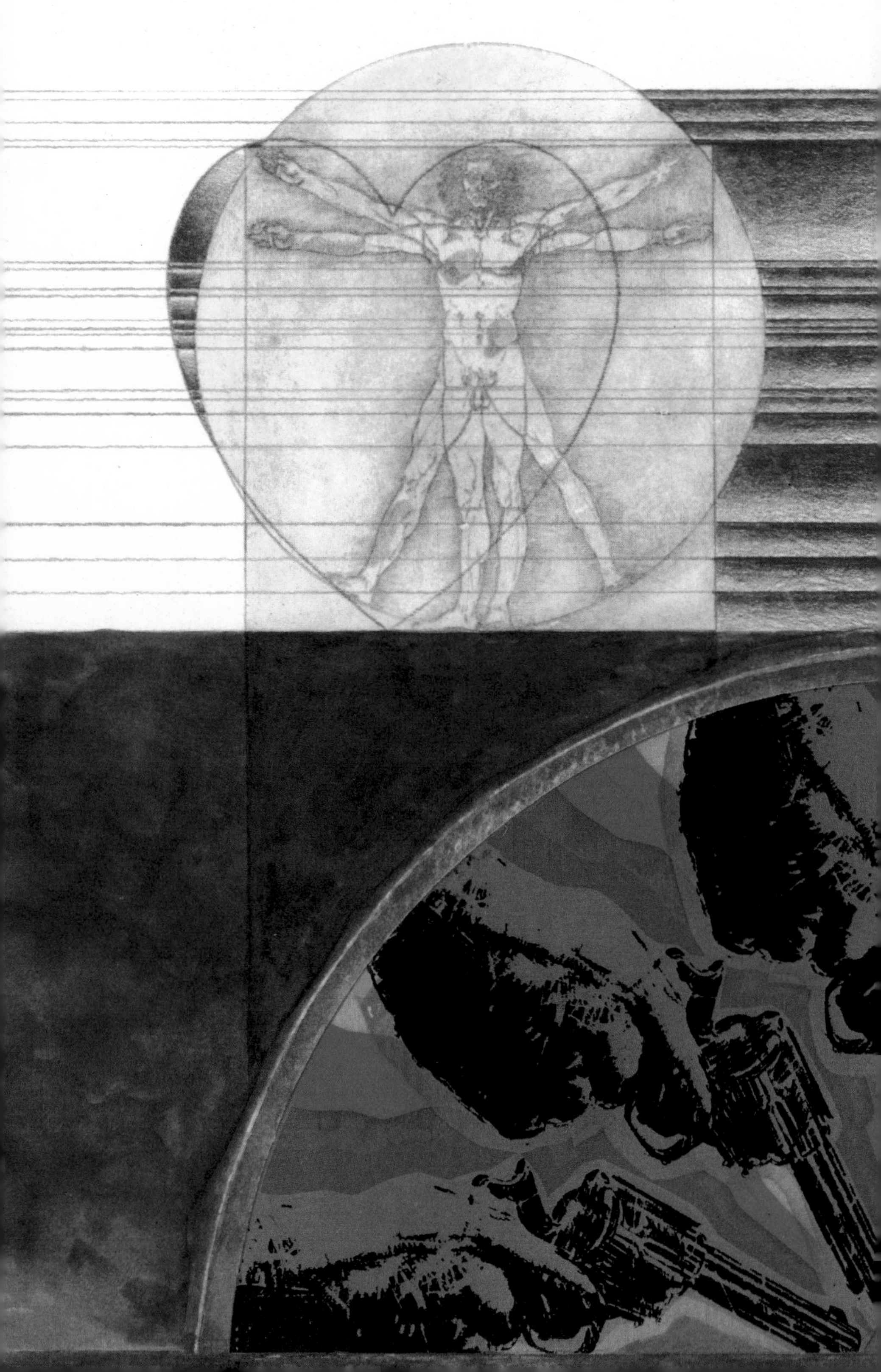

for that love... is the summit of love on earth."

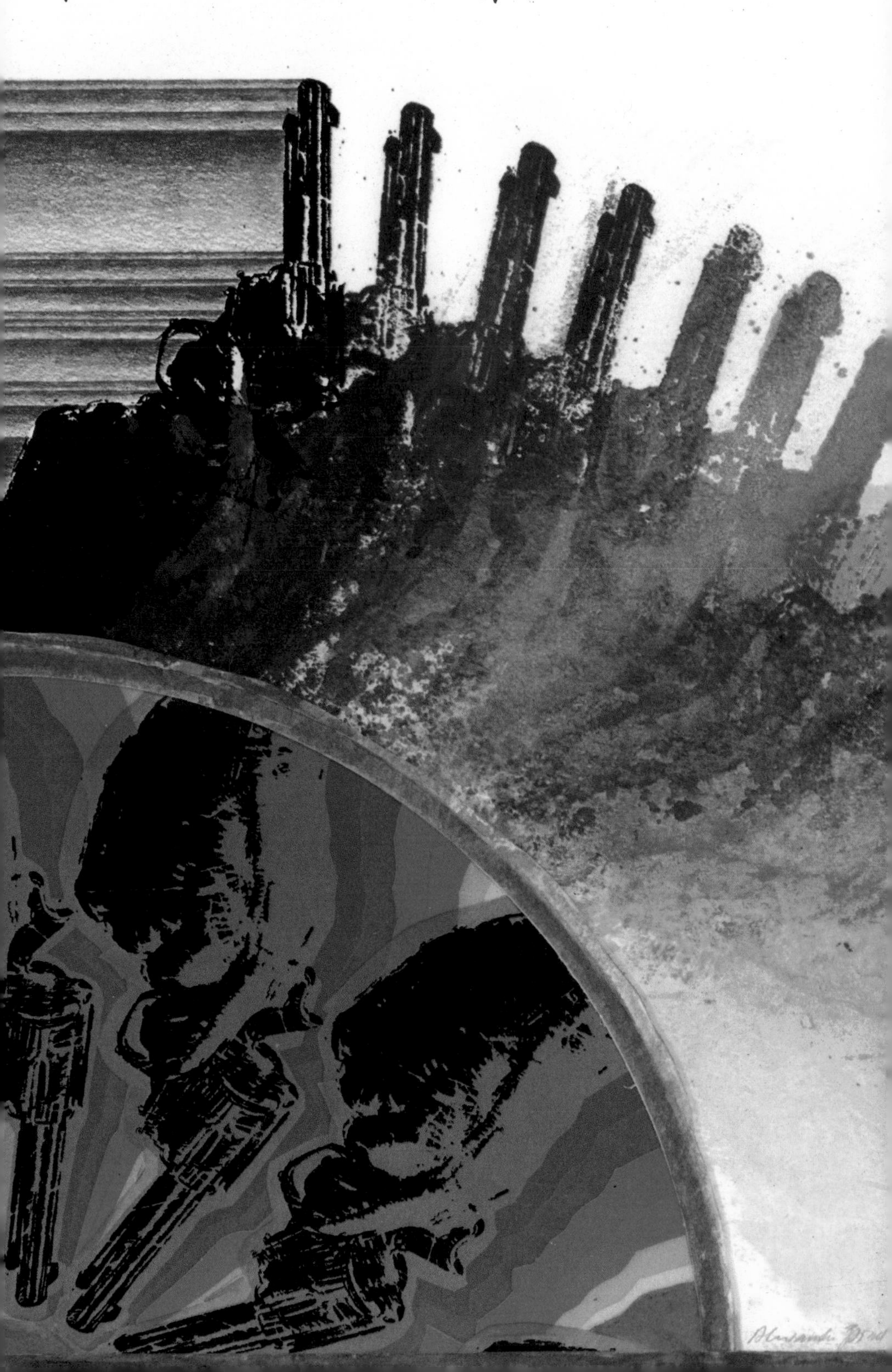

LOVE
PLAYWRIGHT
PLAYWRIGHT

No one says it's

simple

easy

effortless

a breeze...

...and yet to understand the blessing of selfless love...

...to cherish the essence of each individual...

...is to know an inner joy beyond words.

Only so long as we can love one another

can we be truly alive...

...can we be truly happy...

...can we truly anticipate tomorrow.

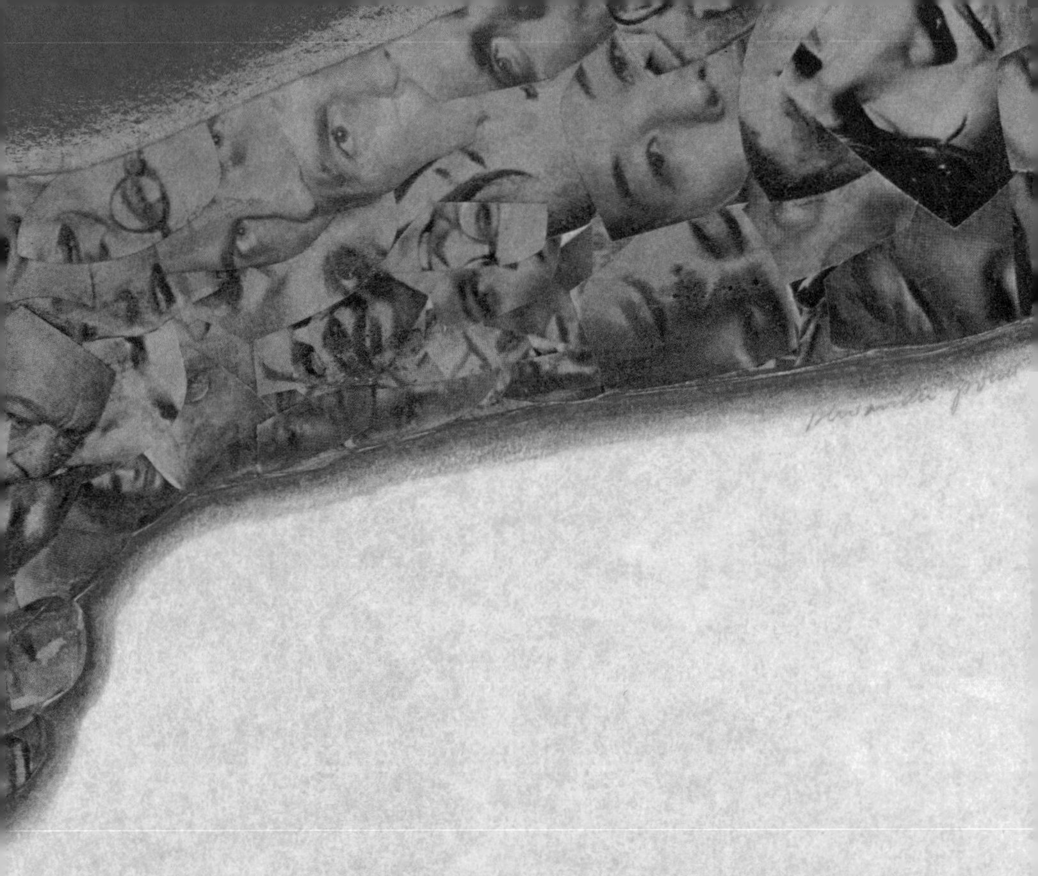

and do you know the final truth by which

Brotherhood will be understood?

Mahatma Gandhi said, "Peace between countries

must rest on the solid foundation of love

between individuals."

We share this world...

...as we share the treasure of each other.

We can move closer together

by our human hands

working toward

a common goal...

...our minds thinking toward

common ideals...

.our hearts loving

toward a common

existence...

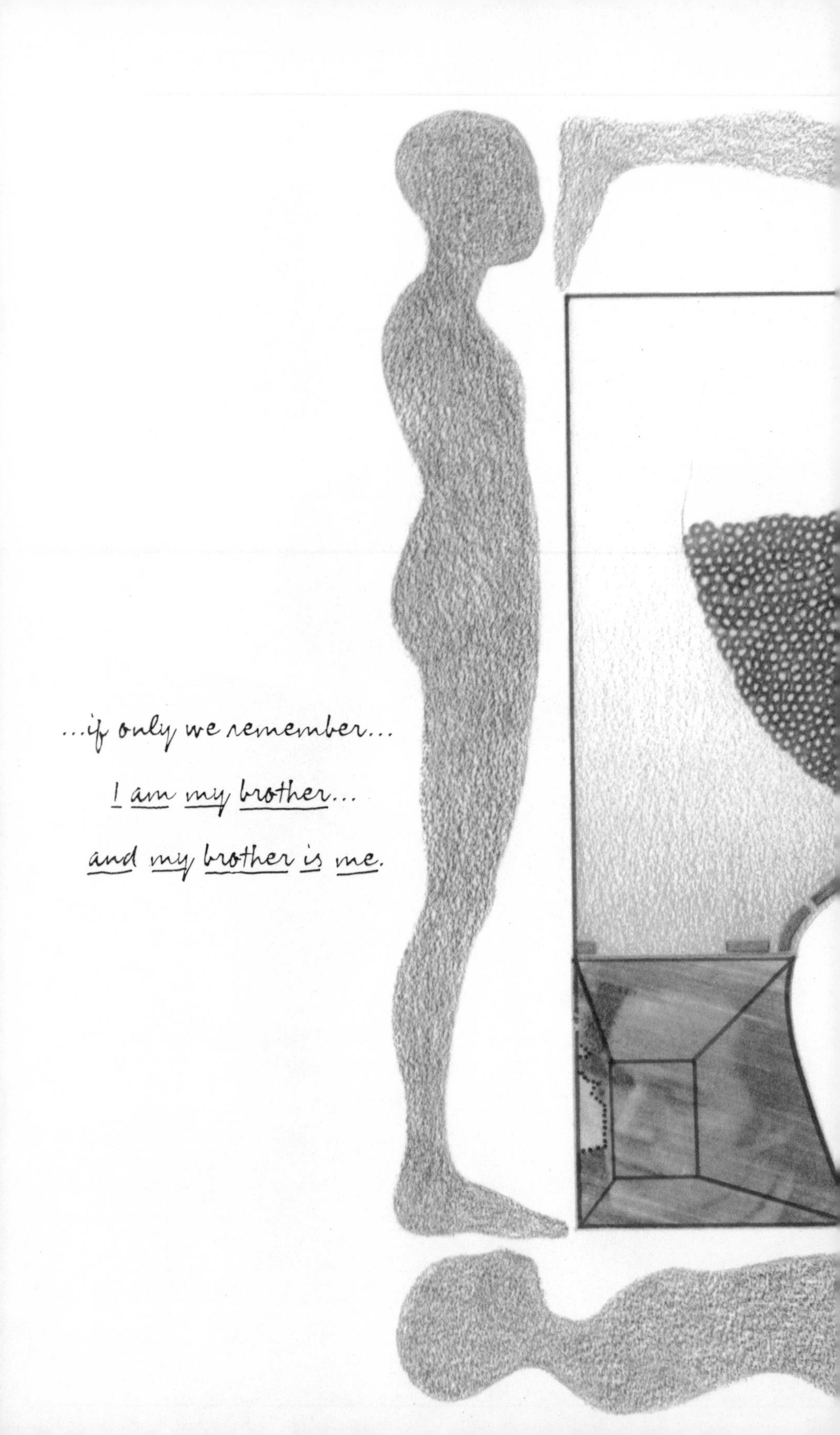
...if only we remember...
I am my brother...
and my brother is me.

The illustrations in this book
are executed in collage,
a creative technique
utilizing all forms of papers,
printed imagery and drawing.
The cover is bound with
natural weave book cloth
and Torino paper.
Inside pages are Hallclear,
White Imitation Parchment
and Ivory Fiesta Parchment.
Book design by Jay Johnson.
The designer gratefully acknowledges
the assistance of Gary Peltier
and Joe Van Dolah
in preparing this edition.

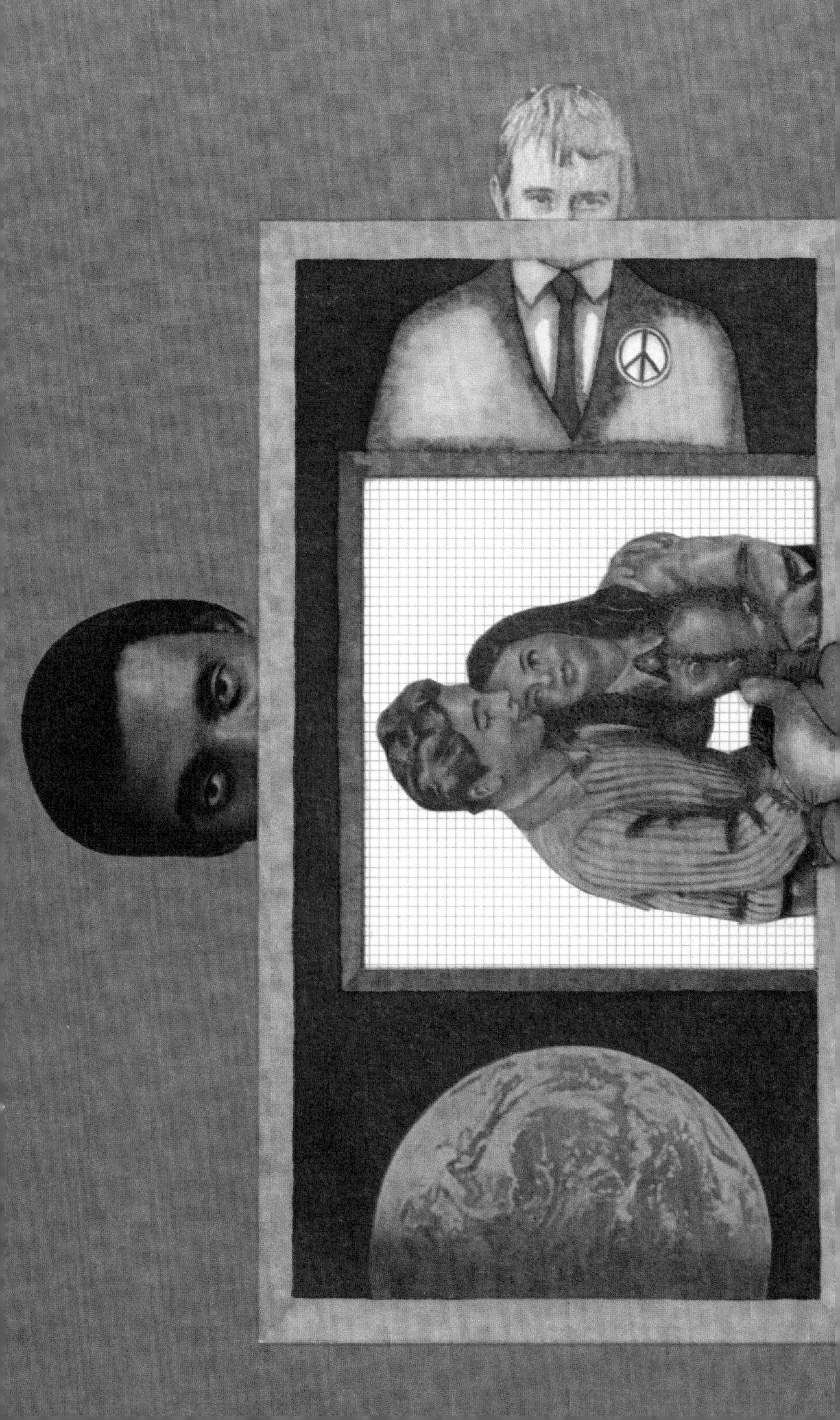